Introduction

An unlimited no-contract cell phone company, also called prepaid cell phone company, is one that provides reasonably priced monthly cell phone plans that involve services with features without limitations. This type of cell phone service is received after subscribers pay a monthly plan of their choice. They may purchase a cell phone of their choice without the influence of a credit check or a contract. Monthly bills involving unlimited no-contract cell phone service are paid at an authorized retailer or store with cash, debit or credit card; they may also be paid in the mail with a payment stub, a check, or money order. Monthly cell phone bills can also be paid over the phone using a credit card, as well as, on the internet using a debit or credit card or a bank or credit union account. The date in which the

1

cell phone bill is due each month is always on the same date a person's cell phone service was activated.

If customers are not impressed by that type of cell phone company, they can try most of the same unlimited features and services with the alternative type of cell phone company known as an unlimited contract cell phone company. An unlimited contract cell phone company is a cell phone company that provides expensive monthly plans that involve services and features with no limitations such as internet, calling, texting, and voicemail. This type of cell phone service requires an agreement with a contract cell phone company for a certain amount of time when a subscriber purchases a cell phone. With a cell phone contract in place, some of the features in a subscriber's cell phone service are chosen separately, and a subscriber's mobile phone internet service is limited at most contract cell phone companies. Also, credit checks are performed, and activation fees are charged before a person's cell phone service is activated. Although the payments of the cell phone bills are done in the same ways no-contract cell phone bills are done, the date in which contract cell phone bills are due is at the end of each month. If customers are not pleased with the services of the contract cell phone companies, they can have their services deactivated. In order to have the service deactivated, subscribers must pay the high-priced termination fee.

When people purchase their cell phones at the authorized retailers of the nine major no-contract cell phone companies such as MetroPCS, Boost Mobile, Virgin Mobile, Cricket, Simple Mobile, T-Mobile, U.S. Cellular, AT&T, and Verizon Wireless, they get great deals on the phones because they buy them at reduced prices off their retail prices as instant or mail-in rebates. Also, when customers receive cell phone service of this type, they do not sign up for a contract, they do not get charged with activation fees, and they do not pay the remainder of your cell phone's retail price in service fees. People do not get charged with local, state, or federal taxes on their cell phone bills, and people get internet service with absolutely no limitations or overage fees whatsoever. If customers pay their cell phone bills in person at an authorized retailer, they get charged with an in-person payment fee that is very low-priced. No-contract customers only pay a few dollars for phone insurance each month as well as a low-priced deductible for a replacement phone in case of loss, theft, or damages. Subscribers receive great cell phone service without the performance of a credit check or a termination fee in case you want to drop their service. Overall, people are paying cell phone bills that are very intelligently cheap for awesome service.

When people purchase cell phones at the authorized retailers of the five major contract cell phone companies such as Sprint, T-Mobile, U.S. Cellular, AT&T, and Verizon Wireless, they receive great deals on the phones because phones are bought at reduced prices off their retail prices. However, they have to commit to a contract that lasts for a couple years. Also, when people pay monthly cell phone bills, they get charged with extremely high service fees, which mean that they are paying the remainder of their cell phones' retail prices. Although cell phone subscribers do not get charged with in-person payment fees when paying in their companies' authorized dealers, they get charged with local, state, and federal taxes. Plus, if people want to have a higher amount of internet usage, also known as data, they have to pay more money for it, thus upgrading their internet services. If people go over the amount of data they have, they get charged with overage fees. When it comes with insurance, they get charged with more money for it each month, and people have to pay a high deductible for replacement phones if their cell phones are stolen, lost, or damaged. In the end, despite receiving great coverage, people are idiotically spending unnecessary amounts of money for unlimited contract monthly plans that do not make sense. When it comes with cell phone deals, unlimited plans, services and features, insurance, and fees, the unlimited no-contract cell phone companies are more intelligent and greater than unlimited contract cell phone companies.

Cell Phone Deals: Unlimited No Contract Cell Phones

Cell phone deals involving unlimited no-contract service are excellent and intelligent to the purchaser. The purchaser doesn't have to have his or her credit checked or sign a long-term contract in order to get great deals on the cell phone he or she chooses. Cell Phone deals include sales, instant or mail-in rebates and special offers. MetroPCS, the fifth largest cell phone company and one of the major no-contract cell phone companies in the United States, always has great deals on their cell phones, plus they provide great offers to people who buy the cell phones. According to the MetroPCS website, when people buy any of the Android cell phones involving MetroPCS service (online or at a MetroPCS store), they get unlimited music from Rhapsody for up to ninety days. In addition to the Rhapsody offer, they get up to a hundred dollars ($100) in mail-in rebates (which comes in MetroPCS Visa prepaid cards) off their cell phones' retail prices. For example, according to the phone list page of the MetroPCS website, the 4G LTE-powered Samsung Galaxy Indulge Android cell phone normally costs $299 when people buy it online or at the MetroPCS retailers. However, after the $100 mail-in rebate and with the unlimited Rhapsody offer, the final price for the Samsung Galaxy Indulge is $199. MetroPCS's newest 4G LTE-powered Android phone, the LG Esteem (which normally costs $349 when bought) is $249 after the $100 mail-in rebate and with the unlimited Rhapsody offer. The Samsung Admire and the Samsung Admire Red Android phones are also great examples of cell phones with additional offers. Both of the Samsung Admires, which retail prices are $129 when they are bought, are marked fifty dollars off after the mail-in rebates and with unlimited music from Rhapsody, and the purchaser of those phones gets $15 worth of free Android applications by mail.

Except MetroPCS's first 4G-LTE smartphone, the Samsung Craft, Blackberry Curve, and Samsung Messager III, all MetroPCS non-Android phones also include mail-in rebates. The final price of the Samsung Freeform III cell phone is $19 after the mail-in rebate, which is thirty dollars off their retail price of $49. Also, the final price of the Huawei M735 Blue is $34 after the $25 mail-in rebate off its retail price of $59.

Unlimited no-contract cell phone companies also offer great deals on their phones when people buy them online. For instance, Boost Mobile has an online promotional discount when people buy one of their phones on their website with the exception of the Samsung Transform Ultra Android cell phone. According to the Boost Mobile website, if they type in the promo code HALLOWEEN20 when they purchase their cell phones, customers get twenty percent off their regular prices through November 1, 2011. For example, if you buy the

Samsung Prevail on the Boost Mobile website and you type in HALLOWEEN20 at checkout, you get the discounted price of $119.99 which is $30 off the regular price of $149.99 for that phone.

Cricket is another unlimited no-contract cell phone company that has great deals on cell phones. When a person buys a cell phone at the Cricket authorized stores or on the Cricket website, he or she gets a discount for their phones. For example, the ZTE Score Android cell phone, when bought online, costs $79.99, $50 off the retail price of $129.99. The Samsung Chrono, when bought online, costs ten dollar less than the retail price of $39.99. MetroPCS, Boost Mobile, and Cricket are not the only unlimited no-contract cell phone companies with great deals on their phones.

Four of the five major unlimited contract cell phone companies have its unlimited no-contract versions that involve great discounts with great service. T-Mobile, although it is mainly known as an unlimited contract cell phone company, is also an unlimited no-contract cell phone carrier; according to the Monthly4G plan page of the T-Mobile website, there's no credit check or a contract to sign when buying a cell phone involving unlimited service. When it comes to no-contract circumstances, T-Mobile has discounts on some of its phones. They offer instant discounts on its participating phones for a limited time. For example, the LG Optimus T Android cell phone, when bought at a T-Mobile retailer or on the T-Mobile website, is instantly discounted at $149.99, which is $37.50 off its retail price of $187.49. T-Mobile also has refurbished discounts on a couple of its cell phones. The refurbished T-Mobile Comet Android cell phone is normally priced at $124.99, but discounted at $99.99.

U.S. Cellular, recognized as a contract cell phone company, has great deals for its cell phones involving unlimited no-contract service. According to the U.S.

Cellular website, the LG Optimus U Android cell phone, which is regularly priced at $249.99, is discounted at $139.99. The HTC Merge Android cell phone is $299.99, which is a $150 prepaid discount from the cell phone's retail price of $449.99. The blue Samsung Character is regularly priced at $199.99. However, with the $90 prepaid discount and the $50 mail-in rebate that comes as a MasterCard debit card, the final price of the phone is $59.99.

AT&T, known mainly as an unlimited contract cell phone company, is a very intelligent unlimited no-contract cell phone company known as GoPhone. It has great discounts on their phones without credit checks or contracts, including refurbished and online discounts. According to the prepaid package page of the AT&T website, The Samsung Solstice II, which is normally priced at $239.99, is marked $170.00 off because it is refurbished. Therefore, a person who chooses it is paying seventy dollars for it. Also, the Samsung Strive GoPhone is discounted online at $119.99, which is $70 off the retail price of $189.99.

Verizon Wireless, another contract cell phone company, has great deals on its unlimited no-contract cell phones in terms of prices, including its basic phones and smartphones. According to the Prepaid page of the Verizon Wireless website, the Samsung Gusto (a basic phone), which is regularly priced at $199.99, is priced at $19.99 when bought at the Verizon website or the company's authorized retailers. The Droid X2 by Motorola (an Android cell phone), which is regularly priced at $449.99, is bought for $294.99 online or at a Verizon retailer. Unlimited no-contract cell phone deals are very blessing and clever to purchasers because after they buy the cell phones, they are not paying the remainder of their cell phones' retail prices in service fees.

Cell Phone Deals: Contract Cell Phones

Cell phone deals involving money off the retail prices are good, but idiotic when unlimited contract service is involved. When buying a cell phone from any of the five major contract cell phone carriers, the purchaser has to have his or her credit check. Along with the performance of a credit check, the person is required to sign a contract for cell phone service, which usually lasts for two years. Contract cell phone deals include instant savings and discounts, web specials, mail-in rebates, and money off the retail prices.

Sprint, one of the five major contract cell phone companies, is known for having great deals on their cell phones. Although all of its cell phones involve two-year contracts, they include big savings from their regular prices. For example, according to the Sprint website, the Kyocera Brio cell phone is normally sold at $219.99, but it is sold at $50.00 when bought at a Sprint retailer. If bought on the Sprint website, the Kyocera Brio is free with a web special. The LG Optimus S Android cell phone, which is normally priced at $299, is discounted at $69.99 at Sprint stores, but is free with a web special. The first IPhone in the history of Sprint, the 16 GB IPhone 4S is regularly priced at $649.99. However, although it does not have a web special, it is sold at Sprint retailers and online for $199.99.

T-Mobile is also known to have fantastic deals on their cell phones, which include mail-in rebates, instant, refurbished, and web discounts. According to the T-Mobile website, the HTC Sensation 4G Android phone is priced regularly at $499.99, but is low-priced at $199.99 with the $250 instant rebate and after the $50 mail-in rebate. The T-Mobile Sidekick 4G is another phone with great deals included. The cell phone subscriber saves $350 off the retail price of that cell phone with the instant, web, and refurnished discounts when buying it online. If bought at a T-Mobile store, the purchaser of the T-Mobile Sidekick 4G can save $270.

U.S Cellular is another major contract cell phone that includes great deals on its cell phones. With contract service, cell phone subscribers of U.S. Cellular (current or first-time) can get some of the phones for free. Also, some of its other cell phones include mail-in rebates. For instance, the LG Saber phone, which costs $159.99, is free with contract agreement. The HTC Wildlife S Android cell phone is regularly priced at $329.99, but is free with the $230 contract discount and after the $100 mail-in rebate. Those and all other cell phones at U.S. Cellular are bought on their website as well as at their authorized dealers in places like Chicago and Dallas.

AT&T, the fourth of the five major contract cell phone companies, has great deals on its cell phones, including web and instant discounts. The AT&T Impulse 4G Android cell phone regularly costs $379.99, but is marked $350 off with a two-year contract. The Sharp FX touchscreen cell phone is regularly priced at $269.99, but with a two-year contract and the $40 refurbished discount, it is priced at $9.99.

Verizon Wireless, America's most trusted contract cell phone company, has great deals on their phones. With the purchase of its cell phones, a person can save a lot of money in terms of online discounts and rebates. For instance, a person can go to the Verizon website and buy the 4G-LTE-powered Pantera Breakout Android cell phone for $99.99 with a two-year contract and the $50 online discount. Plus, he or she saves $260 off their cell phone's retail price of $359.99. When bought in person, the $409.99 4G LTE-powered Samsung Stratosphere Android phone costs a contract price of $199.99. When bought online, it's fifty dollars off at $149.99. Contract cell phone plans may be good, but in the long run, you are paying the remaining

parts of your cell phone's retail price in high service fees.

Monthly Plans: Unlimited No Contract Cell Phone Companies

Unlimited monthly plans involving no-contract cell phone services and features are extremely intelligent, excellent, and sensibly low-priced. Firstly, people who are or get on unlimited monthly plans do not sign up for a long-term contract with their cell phone companies. Secondly, people no-contract monthly plans get most, if not all, of the services and features available to them without limitations; they don't pay separately for major cell phone services such as calling, text-messaging, and internet. Thirdly, when it comes to service with unlimited no-contract cell phone companies, add-on features and subscriptions are smart and cheap to people's unlimited monthly plans. Add-on features and subscriptions involving cell phone service of this kind usually come in bundles. Finally, the nationwide coverage of a person's no-contract cell phone company is great.

MetroPCS is the only no-contract cell phone company in America that have four unlimited monthly plans that range from $40 to $60 and include major services and features such as calling, text-messaging, internet, voicemail, and picture-messaging. According to the plan page of the MetroPCS website, with a $40 monthly plan with MetroPCS, current and new customers get unlimited calling, text-messaging, internet, also known as MetroWeb, and picture-messaging. Also on the $40 plan, people receive a voicemail package, which includes caller ID, call waiting, and three-way calling. MetroPCS also has additional features on their $45, $50, and $60 unlimited monthly plans. With a $45 monthly plan, MetroPCS customers receive unlimited international text messaging, short codes & alerts, premium directory assistance known as Metro411, and Screen-it. Screen-it is a MetroPCS unlimited feature that, according to the MetroPCS website, "allows you to manage incoming calls better by seeing the caller's name before answering the call – it may be a call you would like to miss." It also displays the names of the businesses and people who are calling, including people customers do not know. Screen-it, along with other unlimited features included on the $45 plan, is on the $50 and $60 monthly plans.

On the $50 monthly plan, customers receive unlimited GPS, better known as MetroNavigator, unlimited email access, and unlimited instant messaging. Also on the $50 monthly plan, people receive unlimited Loopt, a feature that, according to the "Learn about MetroPCS Wireless Service" page on the MetroPCS website, "uses GPS technology to automatically share your real-time location with your friends so you do not always have to tell them where you are." In other words, it connects a person to the people, events, and places in his or her surroundings. The $50 monthly plan includes visual voicemail, a feature in which MetroPCS customers have the power to see voicemail details and hear voicemail messages in any order they want on their cell phone. Visual voicemail, along with other additional features on this monthly plan, is also included on the $60 unlimited monthly plan.

On the $60 monthly plan, people receive Visual Voice Mail Plus, a feature in which subscribers can convert their voicemail messages into text messages. According to the "Voice Mail to Text" section of the MetroPCS website, this feature includes messages delivered by email or text, and has the ability to block profane words. Also, customers subscribing to the $60 plan receive a free unlimited application called Pocket Express. As explained on the "Pocket Express: Your Mobile Source for Information" section of the MetroPCS website, Pocket Express stores every piece of the most desired parts of a person's life in one place for him or her to manage on his or her cell phone. The most desired parts of a customer's life include sports, news, weather, maps, travel, info, showbiz, and extras.

Lastly, on this monthly plan, people receive unlimited music from Rhapsody. This monthly plan is available for Blackberry and Android phones. The $50 monthly plan is available for Android cell phones, while the $40, $45, and $50 plans are available for non-smartphones.

The four monthly plans involving MetroPCS service are not the only monthly plans in existence with America's fifth largest cell phone company. In 2010, MetroPCS became the first cell phone company in the United States to launch 4G LTE services, as mentioned on the CNET article, "MetroPCS launches first 4G LTE Market and Phone," by Marguerite Reardon. Since their historic achievement, MetroPCS also has three unlimited 4G LTE monthly plans that range from $40 to $60 and involve the same services and features as the normal unlimited monthly plans. However, the monthly plans involve 4G services. 4G is the fourth generation of mobile technology in which internet browsing, multimedia applications, and features are as fast as a coyote; LTE stands for Long Term Evolution, according to the 4G LTE FAQs page of the MetroPCS website. When people subscribe to the $40 4G LTE unlimited plan, the features and services are similar to the normal $40 unlimited plan, except they receive unlimited web in 4G speeds, which is included on all 4G LTE plans, and 100 MB of multimedia streaming access. On the $50 4G LTE unlimited plan, besides the similarity of the features and services on this plan to its normal counterparts, one GB of multimedia streaming access is received. When people are on the $60 4G LTE monthly plan, they receive unlimited multimedia streaming access, plus they can use MetroSTUDIO Video On Demand, where customers can watch their favorite television shows such as Law & Order SVU, Hell's Kitchen, Kitchen Nightnares, and Cougar Town. 4G coverage is available in 14 market areas including Detroit, Ann Arbor, Warren, Boston, Los Angeles, New York,

Dallas, and South Florida. Although 4G coverage is not available in places like Flint, Grand Blanc, Goodrich, Burton, Chicago, Pittsburgh, and Newark, subscribers can still use their 4G services and features on MetroPCS's 3G Nationwide coverage, which is available in 90 percent of the United States. MetroPCS's three 4G LTE unlimited monthly plans are available for its three 4G LTE phones, including the world's first ever 4G LTE phone, the Samsung Craft, the Samsung Galaxy Indulge Android phone, and the LG Esteem Android phone.

MetroPCS also offers unlimited monthly family plans in which people in each family can receive $5 off their monthly bills with up to five lines. For example, if a family of two chooses the $40 regular unlimited monthly plan, they receive $5 off their bills with two lines, meaning they will be paying $70. If two family members choose the $45 plan and the third family member choose the $60 4G LTE monthly plan, then the family of three will receive $15 off their monthly bill. When it comes to paying bills, they will be paying $135 as a family. All unlimited monthly plans are available on the MetroPCS family plan.

MetroPCS offers additional monthly subscriptions for its customers in low prices, including features that come in bundles. Ringback Tones is a music subscription bundle in which customers receive two ringback tones for only five dollars a month. The second music subscription bundle is called Ringtones Bundle. For also five dollars a month, MetroPCS customers can receive five ringtones in which they can download from their MetroPCS cell phones. The last music subscription bundle for MetroPCS is the Full-track Download Bundle, in which customers can download five full-track songs for five bucks a month. The Roaming Subscription includes the TravelTalk Bundle. TravelTalk is a MetroPCS feature that enables customers to utilize their cell phones outside of their nationwide coverage locations. For five dollars a month, people can make calls while they travel to cities and towns that are not covered by MetroPCS. Text messaging is free with TravelTalk.

In addition to their monthly subscriptions, MetroPCS has additional monthly add-on features for customers in low prices. Corporate Email is an add-on feature in which customers with MetroPCS Blackberry cell phones and plans can access their email accounts for their business for five dollars a month. Unlimited Mexico is a five-dollar monthly add-on feature in which customers on $50, $60 Blackberry, $50 4G LTE, and $60 4G LTE plans can make limitless calls to anyone in Mexico. International Long Distance is a monthly add-on calling feature in which customers have the power to make unlimited calls to anyone in over 1,000 global areas for just ten dollars. The add-on calling feature is also available for cell phones involving the $50, $60 Blackberry, $50 4G LTE, and $60 4G LTE plans. Finally, the Rhapsody unlimited music, another add-on feature, is available to people on the $60 4G

LTE monthly plan for ten dollars. Overall with MetroPCS, people are paying reasonable cell phone bills for unlimited services and features that are great and worth enjoying without the influence of a single contract.

Boost Mobile, second of eight major no-contract cell phone companies, also has unlimited monthly plans for their cell phones. The exception when it comes to monthly plans is that Boost Mobile is the only cell phone company that lowers its customers' bills for every six months that they pay on time. As mentioned on the Boost Mobile website, this process is known as Shrinkage. Current and new Boost Mobile customers who choose the $50 unlimited plan gets their cell phone bill lowered by five dollars for every six on-time payments. After the first six months, customers are paying $45 a month. After the second six-month period, the monthly bills involving Boost Mobile service is $40. After the third and final six-month period, the customers are paying $35 a month for their services.

Shrinkage also applies to the Blackberry and Android monthly plans. When people subscribe to the Blackberry or Android unlimited monthly plans, they start off with payments of $60 for the first six months. Afterwards, their cell phone bills get reduced to $55 a month, which is paid throughout the next six months. When the customers have had the same unlimited plans for a year, the monthly bill will become $50. After customers have had over 18 months of Boost Mobile service, their Blackberry and Android cell phone bills are reduced to a new monthly amount of $45 a month. All three unlimited cell phone plans include calling, text-messaging, picture-messaging, video-messaging, audio-messaging, internet, 411, voicemail, call waiting, and long-distance. The regular unlimited monthly plan includes Nationwide Boost Walkie-Talkie, which is available with IDEN Series phones. Walkie-Talkie is a feature that connects a Boost Mobile subscriber to other Boost Mobile or Nextel customers in the United States. International

Walkie Talkie is also available from the U. S. to Canada, Mexico, Chile, and the rest of Latin America. International Walkie-Talkie rates range from ten to forty cents a minute. The Blackberry monthly plan includes access to the Blackberry App World, while the Android monthly plan features access to the Android Market.

Boost Mobile also has additional monthly features for customers at affordably low prices. International Connect is a feature in which Boost Mobile customers pay five dollars a month to text people worldwide and call people on landlines in Mexico with no limitations. If people want to call people in other countries, they can pay ten dollars to subscribe to International Connect Plus, in which people can call 30 countries unlimitedly. In addition to the services and features, you get great coverage since Boost Mobile is a partner carrier of Sprint and is on the Nationwide Sprint Network, which features Sprint's 3G nationwide network, covering over 178 million Americans.

With Boost Mobile service, people are blessed with having great no-contract service, along with paying the cheapest unlimited monthly bills in their lives.

Virgin Mobile, Sprint's second prepaid company, offers three unlimited no-contract monthly plans for cell phone customers. According to Virgin Mobile's United States website, Although all three of its monthly plans involve unlimited text messaging, video messaging, picture messaging, and 3G internet service, two of them include limited calling in terms of minutes. For 35 bucks a month, subscribers can get 300 minutes of calling time. When people get on the $45 unlimited plan, they receive 1200 minutes of calling time. On the $55 monthly plan, Virgin Mobile customers, new and current, receive unlimited calling. Other features on all three Virgin Mobile unlimited monthly plans include email and instant messaging, Google Maps, and Blackberry Maps. International calling with Virgin Mobile is available to over 200 countries. According to the International Rates tab of the Virgin Mobile USA website, talk rates range for two cents to $5.50 a minute. Finally, because Virgin Mobile is also on the Sprint 3G Nationwide Network, customers receive fantastic coverage throughout much of the United States.

Cricket, another no-contract cell phone company, has three monthly plans that include every unlimited service with the exception of calling minutes. According to the Cricket Wireless website, when current and new customers of Cricket choose the $25 monthly plan, they receive 300 calling minutes, which include calling ID, voicemail, call waiting, and 3-way calling, plus unlimited text, video, and picture messaging, and unlimited web. When people subscribe to the $35 monthly plan, they receive 1,000 calling minutes, unlimited text, video, and picture messaging, and unlimited internet. When people subscribe to the $55 Android Muve Plan, they receive unlimited song downloads, ringtones, and ringback tones along with 500 MBs of 3G data. Plus, they receive 1,000 calling minutes, unlimited text, video, and picture messaging. Navigation, which is a GPS feature application, is included on all monthly plans. When it comes to international long-distance, it depends on what country people with Cricket service call. In regards to international text, video, and picture messaging, if you perform any form of messaging to outgoing countries, you get charged ten cents each. Since Cricket covers 278 million Americans, customers can make long-distance calls and texts throughout the United States, including within its roaming locations without any roaming charges.

Simple Mobile is an independent no-contract cell phone company that is known to being, according to the About Simple Mobile page of its website, the rapidest mobile virtual network operator in the world of wireless technology. It is a reseller of T-Mobile, providing people with unlimited monthly plans that include services and features, using GSM technology and Subscriber Identity Module, also known as SIM, cards. In order to receive Simple Mobile service, people must have unlocked GSM cell phones such as Androids, Blackberry phones, Windows-powered cell phones, or IPhones, which they can bring to its retail stores or buy on the websites of its partner retailers, including CompUSA and Circuit City. Also, cell phone users must have a Simple Mobile SIM card, which they can buy at one of its retailers or on its website for $12.99, along with an unlimited monthly plan of their choice. Finally, people insert the Simple Mobile SIM card into the SIM slot of their GSM cell phones, and they are with Simple Mobile.

Simple Mobile has four unlimited monthly cell phone plans, which requires absolutely no credit checks or contracts, according to the Simple Mobile website. People who choose the $40 monthly plan can receive unlimited services and features such as calling and long-distance, text, video, and picture messaging, and internet up to 3G speeds. Also on this plan, people can receive unlimited email, international messaging, voicemail, call waiting, three-way calling and GPS navigation, and stream music and access Facebook, MySpace, and Twitter. When people subscribe to the $60 unlimited monthly plan, the same features and services are included except the speed of people's internet service are 4G and people can stream videos. On the $50 Blackberry monthly plan, customers can receive unlimited calling, text and picture messaging, 3G internet, email, GPS natigation, access to social networks and Blackberry App World, instant messaging and free $5 international long-distance calling, which expires 30 days after new activations. The same features are included on the $60 monthly plan, which includes 4G internet service. If customers want to call long-distance to countries worldwide, they have to buy a Simple Mobile International Long-Distance PIN for ten dollars, as stated on the website's international long-distance page. They can also buy the International Long-Distance Reup card on the Simple Mobile website for the same price. This feature enables customers to call up to 380 countries worldwide. With Simple Mobile service, customers get 3G coverage much of the United States, including in Detroit, Flint, Saginaw, Grand Rapids, Chicago, Las Vegas, New York, Miami, and Dallas; they also get the fastest-growing 4G coverage of all prepaid cell phone companies in the country. Simple Mobile covers many cities such as Dallas, Seattle, Flint, Detroit, Chicago, Boston, Trenton, and Cleveland, and it is doubling its 4G HSPA+ speed from 21 to 42 Mbps. Overall, subscribers are getting amazingly rapid coverage to go along with their cell phone service that is very low-priced.

T-Mobile has five no-contract monthly plans that include different unlimited services and features without any credit checks. For fifteen dollars a month, customers receive unlimited text, although they pay ten cents for each calling minute. For thirty dollars a month, new T-Mobile customers receive unlimited text and 4G internet with 100 calling minutes. This monthly plan allows people to stream videos, movies, TV shows, play online games, access social websites, and video chat. With unlimited internet service, people are allowed to use the first 5 GB in 4G speeds. When customers, current or new, subscribe to the $50 monthly plan, they get unlimited calling, text messaging, and internet with the first 500 MBs up to 4G speeds. They also receive GPS navigation, which is included on the $60 and $70 plans. On the $60 monthly plan, the same unlimited features and services are included, except it enables customers to download applications, music, and games, and the first 2 GB of unlimited data are used in 4G speeds. On the $70 plan, subscribers can stream videos and music, and receive the same features and services with the first 5 GB of unlimited data in 4G speeds. Voicemail, caller

ID, and call waiting features are included in all unlimited monthly plans. 411 directory assistance is available for all monthly plans for $1.99 per call plus airtime, and downloads of ringtones and wallpapers are $1.49 and up. Blackberry Internet Services, a feature for people with Blackberry phones can access the internet and personal email, is available for the $50 and $70 unlimited monthly plans for ten dollars a month. International unlimited calling and text is also available for the $50 and $70 plans for ten dollars a month. People subscribing to this feature can make limitless calls to landlines in over 50 countries, text people in 200 countries unlimited, and make discounted calling and text messages to mobile and landline phones limitlessly. When it comes to international roaming, text messaging costs ten cents for people to send to and receive from Canada. It also costs 50 cents if people want to send text messages to other countries and 10 cents to receive them from other countries. Picture and video messaging are 25 cents to send and receive. International calling rates range from 59 cents to $5.99 for each minute. Also, people receive 96% cell phone coverage throughout the United States with enjoyably low-priced unlimited monthly plan and services with T-Mobile.

U.S. Cellular, although they offer five no-contract monthly plans with unlimited text, video, and picture messaging, has two plans with unlimited calling and no unlimited internet. When new and current U.S. Cellular customers choose the $30 monthly plan, they receive 200 calling minutes, with unlimited messaging and no internet included. For $40 a month, people can receive unlimited messaging with 450 calling minutes and 500 MBs of web. For $50 a month, people can call and message other people in the United States limitless without internet access. People on the $60 monthly plan receive unlimited messaging with 450 calling minutes and 2 GB of web. For seventy dollars a month, U.S. Cellular customers receive unlimited calling and messaging with 2 GB of internet. Three-way calling, caller ID, voicemail, and call waiting are included on all unlimited plans. Any call made outside a U.S. Cellular customer's local calling area is 29 cents a minute. My Contact Backup is a feature for transferring a person's contacts to a new cell phone in case of loss, damage, or theft of his or her current cell phone. It is available on all unlimited no-contract plans. Nationwide coverage in terms of no-contract service with U.S. Cellular is available in few states like Illinois, Kansas, and Oklahoma. Roaming charges may apply.

AT&T has two GoPhone unlimited no-contract plans involving their features and services. For twenty-five dollars a month, people receive unlimited text, instant, video, and picture messaging with 250 minutes of calling, which includes caller ID, voicemail, nationwide long-distance, three-way calling, and call forwarding. If customers want to add data to your $25 monthly unlimited plan, you have to pay $5 for 10 MB, $15 for 100 MB, or $25 for 500 MB. If subscribers want to send message to people internationally, they have to pay twenty five cents for each sent text message and fifty cents for each sent picture and video message. Received text messages internationally are 20 cents each, and received video and picture messaging are twenty-five cents each. For fifty dollars a month, GoPhone subscribers receive unlimited calling, messaging, and data.

If people want to call long-distance to other countries with their AT&T no-contract service, the International Long Distance Feature Package is ten dollars a month. This feature enables customers to call people's landlines in 50-plus countries, including Mexico, Canada, and Jamaica, by using 250 calling minutes. When traveling in Mexico or Canada, roaming charges for text messages are twenty-five cents for each sent message and twenty cents for each received message. Instant messaging roaming charges are fifty cents for each sent and received message. Roaming charges for picture messaging are $1.30 for each sent message and 25 cents for each received message. Internet browsing (data) is nearly two cents for each KB. Calls made or received while traveling in Mexico is 25 cents per minute, and voicemails made or received while traveling offshore in the Gulf of Mexico are 99 cents a minute. Calls made or received while traveling in Canada is 40 cents for each minute. There is no daily fee for customers on the $50 unlimited plan with a daily access fee. Overall, you are paying a cheap unlimited phone bill that you don't have to sign up a contract for.

Verizon Wireless has two unlimited no-contract monthly plans involving services and features. According to the Prepaid Plans page of the Verizon website, people with basic cell phones subscribing to the $50 monthly plan receive unlimited calling, messaging, and internet. If people with smartphones choose to have unlimited calling, messaging, and data without any influence of a single contract, they have to pay for them separately since they don't come in a bundled monthly plan. Unlimited calling is $74.99 with an allowance of 25 cents a minute. Unlimited messaging is twenty dollars, and data, which include internet and email, is thirty dollars. Altogether, people are paying $125.00 for unlimited no-contract cell phone service with the most expensive cell phone company of all nine unlimited prepaid cell phone companies in terms of monthly bills.

Although international video and picture messaging is bundled up with unlimited messaging, meaning there are no charges for sending or receiving messaged from Mexico, Puerto Rico, and Canada, according to the website, Verizon charges unlimited prepaid smartphone customers 50 cents for each sent message and 25 cents for each received message when messaging other countries. When texting Canada, Mexico, and Puerto Rico, people with

Verizon prepaid service have to pay 20 cents for each sent and received message. If customers text other countries, they have to pay twenty-five cents for each sent message and twenty cents for each received message. International calling rates range from ten cents to $1.50 for each minute. When roaming to international places, calling rates range from 69 cents to $1.99 per minute, while messaging is 50 cents per sent message and 5 cents per received message. Although customers are paying the highest unlimited no-contract bill for great Verizon service, they are better off not having to pay more for higher amounts of the services they want.

Monthly Plans: Unlimited Contract Cell Phone Companies

Unlimited monthly plans involving contracts are expensive and can be senseless, depending what company people receive service with. Firstly, people who choose monthly plans that involve unlimited services and features must have their credits checked and sign up contracts that last for a pair of years. Secondly, although people get great service and features, some of them may be limited in terms of amounts, and they have to pay extra for higher amounts. When it comes to receiving service with companies like AT&T and Verizon, cell phone users have to pay for calling, messaging, and data features separately since they are not bundled on a single unlimited monthly plan. In the end, people are paying more money for contract cell phone service.

Of all the five major contract cell phone companies in the United States, Sprint has the most intelligent unlimited monthly plan. When current and new Sprint customers choose the Simply Everything plan, they receive unlimited calling, texting, and internet with the $10 Premium data included for the monthly rate of $100.00. According to the Sprint website, with this plan, people can watch the Nascar Sprint Cup races with Nascar Sprint Cup Mobile, check emails, and use GPS navigation. When it comes to international calling, you have to pay five to fifteen dollars a month to call Mexico and other countries. You also have to pay ten dollars a month to send text messages to Mexico and other countries with your Sprint cell phone. When traveling to international places with your Sprint cell phone, with the exception of Mexico, Puerto Rico, and U.S. Virgin Islands, calling rates range from 59 cents to nearly 5 dollars. Messaging rates are fifty cents per sent message and five cents per received message. Other features range from $2.99 to $29.99 a month, and all features and services are also available on the Sprint

Simply Everything Family unlimited plan, which costs $190 a month. Although you get great coverage and service to go along with the U.S.'s smartest postpaid mobile monthly plan, you are still paying slightly more money for your Sprint service.

T-Mobile has four of its five unlimited monthly contract plans that feature different amounts of data, according to its website. Starting at $60 a month, cell phone customers can receive unlimited calling and texting. For $70 a month, customers receive 500 MB of internet data, which people can use to check emails and news. People subscribing to the $80 plan receive 2GB of data, which they can use to browse the web and access social websites. If customers want to use 5GB of data to stream and share videos and entertainment, they have to pay $90 a month. If they want 10GB of data, which downloads music, people have to pay $30 extra a month. People who wish to call and text internationally, the monthly rate is $15. As well as international roaming goes, calling rates vary on what country people are traveling to; text-messaging rates are 20 to 50 cents a sent message and 20 cents a received message. In terms of unlimited monthly family plans, they range from $100 for just calling and texting to $220 for 10 GB of data. Although cell phone customers get 96% nationwide coverage, they are wasting more money for higher amounts of data to add to their unlimited monthly plans.

U.S. Cellular has three major contract monthly plans with unlimited messaging and 5GB of data, although calling minutes vary. According to the U.S. Cellular website, people choosing the $80 monthly plan receive 450 calling minutes, while people get 1200 minutes of calling for $90 a month. If people subscribe to the Simple Line Premium Plus monthly plan, they receive unlimited calling for $110 a month. U.S. Cellular's best-value family plans involve unlimited calling and messaging with different options of data. For $140 a month, family members can call and messaging unlimited, and if they want data, they have to pay $15-$30 extra a month for 50 MB and 5 GB of data. For $160, they receive 5 GB of data. When families choose the monthly plans with U.S. Cellular, they get points and faster phone upgrade as part of its Belief Project. When traveling internationally, only calling rates are available, ranging from 19 cents to two dollars. While U.S. Cellular's coverage is huge, its markets are short and are available in states like Illinois, Oklahoma, and Iowa. Overall, U.S. Cellular contract customers would be paying more for more calling minutes and data on their monthly plans.

There are two contract cell phone companies whose unlimited monthly plans are completely senseless that people have to pay separately for features. AT&T is one example. For seventy dollars a month, customers can call people in the United States limitlessly. If people want to text unlimitedly, they have to pay twenty dollars a month.

If people want data, they have to pay ten to forty-five dollars a month, depending what cell phone they have with AT&T. All other features range from two to twenty dollars a month, including international messaging, which costs $10.00 a month. The features apply to the $50 voice only family plan, which families get unlimited calling for each line. In terms of international roaming, messaging rates of any form range from 50 cents to $1.30 per sent message while the global messaging packages range from ten to fifty dollars a month with overage rates for each message is 15 to 35 cents. Received messages are 25 to 35 cents. Calling rates vary, depending what country customers are traveling to. Although you are getting great coverage, you are paying $70 to $135 a month for AT&T cell phone service.

Verizon Wireless is the other example of a contract cell phone company that people have to pay separately for unlimited calling and texting with different amounts of data. If Verizon customers choose the Single-Line Plan, as shown on the company's website, they have to pay

separately for unlimited calling for seventy dollars a month

and unlimited messaging for $20 a month. Data amounts

ranging from 2 GB to 12 GB are $30 to $100 a month,

meaning people are paying $70 to $190 monthly for

Verizon cell phone service. If customers go over the

amount of data they are allowed to use, they get charged

ten dollars for each GB. The data prices also apply on the

family plan, which include unlimited calling for $120 and

unlimited texting for $30. If you travel internationally, the

text messaging rates are 20-25 cents per sent message and

25 cents per received message. Video and picture

messaging rates are 25-50 cents per sent message and 25

cents per received message. International calling roaming

rates start at 6 cents a minute for the value plan and 39

cents a minute for the standard plan. Global Data amounts

from 50 MB to 300 MB cost $30 to $125 a month.

Although subscribers get perhaps the largest nationwide

coverage with Verizon Wireless, they are paying the most expensive cell phone bill of their lives. Overall, with postpaid unlimited service, people would be paying extremely high cell phone bills.

Fees and Deductibles: Unlimited No Contract Cell Phone Service

Fees and phone insurance are the things people have to deal with when having cell phone service. In terms of unlimited no-contract cell phone service, some companies may charge payment fees when paying in their retailers and over the phone. Phone insurance regarding unlimited prepaid cell phone service, it is cheap, and the deductibles depend what cell phones are lost, stolen, or damaged. According to the MetroPCS Bill Pay Overview page of the website, MetroPCS customers are charged are $3.00 in-person fee when paying in their retailers; some MetroPCS retailers may charge an extra $2.00 fee with use of a debit card other than the MetroPCS Visa Debit Card. When people pay their MetroPCS bill over the phone, they are charged with a $3 payment fee. In terms of insurance, according to the Learn about MetroPCS Wireless Service Features page, MetroPCS charges customers $6 a month to protect their calling contacts and cell phones from damage, loss, or theft. In case if any of the three factors happens, people must pay a $19-$139 deductible to get a replacement cell phone.

Cricket Wireless's in-person payment fee is $3.00 when paying cell phone bills at a Cricket retailer, according to its website. When Cricket customers pay over the phone with one of the cell phone company's representative, they are charged with $3; customers are charged with a two-dollar over-the-phone payment fee when paying monthly bills on an automated system over the phone. Insurance involving Cricket service are $5 a month, and deductibles, in case of theft, damage, or loss, and depending what cell phone a person has, range from $20-$150.

In terms of payment fees, according to the email interview, since Boost Mobile has independent dealers, in-person and over-the-phone payment fees vary. However, the cell phone insurance regarding Boost Mobile service is five dollars a month. In case of loss, damage, or theft, the deductibles range from $20 to $100. Virgin Mobile's in-person payment fees vary in terms of what stores people go to pay their bills at, according to the email interview. The company includes over-the-phone charges on the monthly bills as service taxes. The cell phone insurance involving Virgin Mobile service is five dollars a month, and the deductibles, according to the Phone Insurance online file, range from $25 to $100. Simple Mobile has independent dealers, according to the email interview, so their in-person fees depend from store to store. There are no over-the-phone payment fees, and there is no insurance since Simple Mobile has a bring-your-phone policy.

Fees and Deductibles: Unlimited Contract Cell Phone Service

Although contract cell phone companies do not charge payment fees when paying in-person or over the phone for prepaid or postpaid service, activation fees and deactivation fees varies depending what type of cell phone service people have. Sprint is the only contract cell phone company that does not charge deactivation fees to customers. It only charges an activation fee of $36, and the cell phone insurance is $8. When it comes to IPhones, Applecare insurance fee is $99. Deductibles to receive replacement basic or smartphone are priced from $50 to $100.

T-Mobile does not charge unlimited prepaid customers any activation fees. However, it charges unlimited contract customers a $35 activation fee for their cell phone service. If people wants to leave T-Mobile, they must pay from $50 to $200 to have their cell phone service deactivated, depending the number of days there are left on their contracts. Cell phone insurance involving T-Mobile service costs between $3.99 and $7.99, according to the email interview. Deductibles range in price from $40 to $130.

There are no activation fees for AT&T unlimited no-contract customers. However, for contract cell phone service, the activation fee is $36, and the deactivation fee is $150-$325 minus $10 for each full completed month of service. Cell phone insurance with AT&T service is seven dollars a month, and deductibles range from $50 to $199.

U.S. Cellular is one of the cell phone companies that charge new unlimited prepaid customers an activation fee, which is $35 to $50. The activation fee for new unlimited contract customers is $30, and the deactivation fee is $150. U.S. Cellular's phone insurance is $5.95 a month, and the deductibles range from $50 to $100, whether or not lost, damaged, or stolen cell phones require data plans.

People choosing unlimited no-contract cell phone service with Verizon Wireless must pay $25 to have their accounts activated. To have contract service, new Verizon customers must pay a $35 activation fee. If people have a basic cell phone with Verizon service and want to have their service deactivated, you must pay $175. The $350 deactivation fee applies to Verizon Wireless subscribers who have smartphones. Insurance range from two to eight dollars a month, and deductibles are $50 to $199. While insurance regarding both types of cell phone service are very reasonable, people may pay much money to get a replacement for their cell phones, which is better than not having cell phone insurance and having to pay full price for the same phone as replacement. While you may be charged with payment fees, having no activation or deactivation fees in terms of no-contract service is a blessing to people.

Flip Side of the Coin: Unlimited Contract Cell Phone Service

Although unlimited contract cell phone service seems high-priced and idiotic, it might be satisfying to people, depending what company or companies they are or have been with and how long they have been with their cell phone companies. People who have been with Sprint are satisfied with its services and features. In an email interview with the University of Michigan-Flint's counselor Dr. Tamara McKay, who is a ten-plus-year Sprint customer, she mentions that the reason she likes Sprint is because it is the only contract cell phone company that provides customers with "true unlimited data." With people having Sprint service, they get to use the kind of internet that is completely infinite, rapid, and free of limits and overage fees. Customers would be totally blessed to use limitless internet data that is bundled in their contract monthly plans. Other contract and no-contract cell phone companies such as Verizon Wireless, AT&T, T-Mobile, and U.S. Cellular, with the exception of MetroPCS, Boost Mobile, Virgin Mobile, Cricket Wireless, and Simple Mobile, do not provide their customers with infinite data that does not slow down, is bundled in monthly plans, or is free of limitations and overage fees. When Dr. McKay was asked what she would think if she had the opposite cell phone service, she stated, "I prefer having an unlimited data plan."

Although having unlimited service with contract cell phone companies are expensive in people's individual or family monthly plans, individual monthly plans with limited features and services can be cheaper and satisfying. For example, Tim Kranz, an UM-Flint drawing instructor, painter, and Verizon Wireless contract customer, stated in the email interview that he gets 400 calling minutes to non-Verizon customers with unlimited Verizon-to-Verizon minutes and limited texting. Although he does not worry about the amount of data he uses with his LG Android phone, his cell phone bill is cheap. Rachel Meehling, a UM-Flint student, stated in an email interview that she currently has a bundled individual monthly plan with Sprint involving unlimited texting with 500 calling minutes and no data. The reason for the talk-plus-text monthly plan that she has with Sprint is that she is more used to maintaining contact with people by texting rather than calling. Therefore she is paying $50 a month for her Sprint service, and she has been with Sprint for two weeks prior to the interview. People on individual plans can have a cheap cell phone bill without having more than one unlimited service and the amount of features needed such as calling minutes.

Family monthly plans can be cheaper, smarter, and advantageous to people, depending how long people have been with their cell phone company and perhaps how long they have had the same cell phones. For example, UM-

Flint's English 112 professor Scott Caddy has been on a family plan with AT&T since 2002, when AT&T Wireless was originally called Cingular Wireless. He received a Nokia Clamshell-style phone when his parents purchased the service. According to the email interview, the cell phone was upgraded in late 2007 to early 2008, which was discounted after rebate. He currently has unlimited data, which costs $20 a month on his family plan and which he uses 1.5 GBs of it. Overall, his family plan is $40 a month with unlimited calling, text messaging, and internet bundled.

Lori Rathbun, a student services specialist at UM-Flint and 10-to-12-year Verizon customer, has a family plan with five people involving 1400 allowable minutes, unlimited texting, and data plan with one people. She has a Verizon EnV, which was discounted, according to her, because she waited a couple years until she got the discount. Although she does not use data, she is blessed with the company's services. When she was asked about the way she feels about Verizon, she stated, "I like Verizon, I personally think phone service is expensive but when you consider all that is literally at your fingertips, I guess it is worth it. My monthly bill is typically the same as I pay for a plan that allows ample time of usage and with 5 people on my plan we do not use half of our hours. However, I would rather pay for too many hours than to go over in hours and be charged astronomical charges." Since Lori has been a Verizon contract customer for over a decade, she gets discounts on accessories she buys, according to her. People who have had contract service with a single cell phone company can receive special offers such as discounts on new phones and accessories and upgrades on old cell phones. Long-time customers have the power to keep their family plans along with their services and features as they were when they first received them. Getting cell phone upgrades and discounts and keeping cell phone plans as cheap as before are like getting a new paint job on a person's vehicle and still keeping the car insurance low-priced.

Contract cell phone insurance involving deductibles are high-priced, but not having cell phone insurance regarding this type of service can be advantageous after all. Kristen Matthias, a seven-year AT&T customer and a program coordinator of UM-Flint's Women's Educational Center, has no insurance on her I-Phone. However, when she has experience in going through several I-Phones because of loss and damage, she buys a low-priced refurbished version of her phone. She stated in the email interview, "It is a much better deal, and the phones are like new." People do not have to have insurance on their cell phones and pay expensive deductibles for replacements if their phones are misplaced, damaged, or stolen. Contract cell phone customers can purchase pre-owned or refurbished versions of their cell phones as replacements instead of paying full price for newer versions. When it comes to contract cell phone service, people can take advantages of the special offers their companies provide them, including discounted phones, upgraded phones without any changes on monthly plans, low-priced monthly plans with necessary amounts of minutes, messages, and data, and discounted pre-owned phones without paying full price for replacements due to loss, theft, or damage. As long as customers manage the amounts of services they use, they are blessed to be under mobile phone contracts. Even if they pay high-priced cell phone bills, as long as they are presented with great offers, it is worth the money and the blessing.

Conclusion

People can go purchase cell phones at the stores or on the websites they choose and get money off their cell phones' retail prices in instant and mail-in rebates and discounts. However, the deals people take advantage of when buying cell phones depends on the types of cell phone service they involve. People purchasing low-priced and discounted cell phones receive unlimited no-contract service with companies like MetroPCS, Boost Mobile, Virgin Mobile, Cricket Wireless, Simple Mobile, T-Mobile, U.S. Cellular, AT&T, and Verizon Wireless. With this type of cell phone service, customers pay less money for the monthly plans that include most of the unlimited services and features being bundled together; a couple of the services such as calling and internet may be limited on a people's monthly plans, depending on the no-contract cell phone companies they are with. Most no-contract cell phone companies do not charge customers with activation fees, but they all do not charge people with deactivation fees. Although most of the no-contract cell phone companies offer reasonably priced insurance with moderately priced deductibles, they all have great coverage people can enjoy without signing up for long-term contracts or paying more for more amounts of the same services.

When people take advantage of the cell phone deals at the stores or on the websites of the five postpaid cell phone companies like Sprint, T-Mobile, U.S. Cellular, AT&T, and Verizon Wireless, they have to sign up for long-term contracts, meaning they get locked up in binding agreements like they are prisoners. People receive high-priced monthly plans with some, if not most, services and features that are limitless in amounts and bundled with their cell phone plans. Depending what company people have contract cell phone service with, they receive limited amounts of internet service in which they have to pay separately for and pay more money to receive more amounts. In the meantime, people end up paying overage charges for their internet when they use more than the amount they pay to use, which results in ridiculously high-priced cell phone bills. Although people do not get charged with any form of payment fees when paying cell phone bills at their contract companies' authorized dealers, they have to deal with local, state, and federal taxes as well as pricy insurance with moderately priced deductibles. Even though people get charged with activation fees when signing up for service, they get charged with pricey deactivation fees if they are not satisfied with having contract cell phone service. Although they get great service, contract cell phone customers are overall paying cell phone bills that are ridiculously high-priced. If people want to receive the type of cell phone service that includes deals that do not require long-term agreements, intelligently affordable monthly plans with services and features that are completely unlimited and free of overall and deactivation fees, whether they are bundled or separate, and low-priced

fees and insurance along with great coverage, unlimited no-

contract cell phone service is the smarter route to take.

Works Cited

AT&T. "AT&T International - Wireless from AT&T." Cell Phones, Cell Phone Plans, &

    Wireless Accessories - from AT&T. AT&T, 2011.

    Web. 05 Nov. 2011.

AT&T. "AT&T Mobile Insurance." Cell Phones, Cell Phone Plans, & Wireless Accessories –

    from AT&T. AT&T, 2011. Web. 07 Nov. 2011.

AT&T. "Early Termination Fee Policy – Wireless from AT&T." Cell Phones, Cell Phone Plans,

    & Wireless Accessories - from AT&T. AT&T,

    2011. Web. 07 Nov. 2011.

AT&T. "FamilyTalk Nation Unlimited - Get Started - from AT&T." Cell Phones, Cell Phone

    Plans, & Wireless Accessories - from AT&T.

    AT&T, 2011. Web. 05 Nov. 2011.

AT&T. "GoPhone® International Long Distance - Wireless from AT&T." Cell Phones, Cell

Phone Plans, & Wireless Accessories - from AT&T.

AT&T, 2011. Web. 04 Nov. 2011.

AT&T. "GoPhone Plans Get Started - from AT&T." Cell

Phones, Cell Phone Plans, & Wireless

Accessories - from AT&T. AT&T, 2011. Web. 04

Nov. 2011.

AT&T. "Impulse 4G (TM)* by AT&T." Wireless.att.com.

AT&T, 2011. Web. 2 Nov. 2011.

AT&T. "Nation Unlimited - Get Started - from AT&T."

Cell Phones, Cell Phone Plans, &

Wireless Accessories - from AT&T. AT&T, 2011.

Web. 05 Nov. 2011.

AT&T. "Sharp FX (TM) - Refurbished." Wireless.att.com.

AT&T, 2011. Web. 02 Nov. 2011.

AT&T. "Wireless International Rates - Wireless from

AT&T." Cell Phones, Cell Phone Plans, &

Wireless Accessories - from AT&T. AT&T, 2011.

Web. 05 Nov. 2011.

Boost Mobile. "Android Monthly Unlimited | Boost

Mobile." Prepaid Unlimited Cell Phones |

    No Contract Android & Blackberry Plans | Boost

    Mobile. Boost Mobile, 2011. Web. 02 Nov. 2011.

Boost Mobile. "BlackBerry Monthly Unlimited | Boost

Mobile." Prepaid Unlimited Cell Phones |

    No Contract Android & Blackberry Plans | Boost

    Mobile. Boost Mobile, 2011. Web. 02 Nov. 2011.

Boost Mobile. "Boost Mobile - International Rates Walkie-

Talkie." Prepaid Unlimited Cell

    Phones | No Contract Android & Blackberry Plans |

    Boost Mobile. Boost Mobile, 2011. Web. 03 Nov.

    2011.

Boost Mobile. "Boost Mobile Coverage Map | Boost

Mobile." Prepaid Unlimited Cell Phones |

    No Contract Android & Blackberry Plans | Boost

    Mobile. Boost Mobile, 2011. Web. 03 Nov. 2011.

Boost Mobile. "International Connect Cell Phone Service |
Boost Mobile." Prepaid Unlimited

> Cell Phones | No Contract Android & Blackberry
>
> Plans | Boost Mobile. Boost Mobile, 2011. Web. 02
>
> Nov. 2011.

Boost Mobile. "Interview About Payment Fees." Message
to the author. 2 Nov. 2011. E-mail.

Boost Mobile. "Monthly Unlimited | Boost Mobile."
Prepaid Unlimited Cell Phones | No

> Contract Android & Blackberry Plans | Boost
>
> Mobile. Boost Mobile, 2011. Web. 02 Nov. 2011.

Boost Mobile. "Phone Insurance – Protect Your Cell Phone
| Boost Mobile." Prepaid Unlimited

> Cell Phones | No Contract Android & Blackberry
>
> Plans | Boost Mobile. Boost Mobile, 2011. Web. 05
>
> Nov. 2011.

Boost Mobile. "Prepaid Phones – Android, Smartphone,
Qwerty, Camera | Boost Mobile."

Prepaid Unlimited Cell Phones | No Contract
Android & Blackberry Plans | Boost Mobile. Boost
Mobile, 2011. Web. 02 Nov. 2011.

Boost Mobile. "Walkie-Talkie Service – Nationwide Plans |
Boost Mobile." Prepaid Unlimited
Cell Phones | No Contract Android & Blackberry
Plans | Boost Mobile. Boost Mobile, 2011. Web. 03
Nov. 2011.

Cricket Wireless. "$25 Plan - Cell Phone Plan | Cricket
Wireless." Cell Phone Plans | Cell
Phones | Mobile Broadband | Cricket Wireless.
Cricket Wireless, 2011. Web. 03 Nov. 2011.

Cricket Wireless. "$35 Plan - Cell Phone Plan | Cricket
Wireless." Cell Phone Plans | Cell
Phones | Mobile Broadband | Cricket Wireless.
Cricket Wireless, 2011. Web. 03 Nov. 2011.

Cricket Wireless. "$55 Android Muve Plan - Cell Phone
Plan | Cricket Wireless." Cell Phone

Plans | Cell Phones | Mobile Broadband | Cricket
Wireless. Cricket, 2011. Web. 03 Nov. 2011.

Cricket Wireless. "Prepaid Cell Phones | Mobile Phones |
Cricket Wireless." Cell Phone Plans |
Cell Phones | Mobile Broadband | Cricket Wireless.
Cricket Wireless, 2011. Web. 02 Nov. 2011.

Cricket Wireless. "Support | Cricket Wireless." Cell Phone
Plans | Cell Phones | Mobile
Broadband | Cricket Wireless. Cricket Wireless,
2011. Web. 05 Nov. 2011.

Kranz, Tim. "Interview about Your Cell Phone Company,
Service, and History."
Message to the author. 18 Nov. 2011. E-mail.

Matthias, Kristen. "Interview about Your Cell Phone
Company, Service, and History." Message
to the author. 9 Nov. 2011. E-mail.

McKay, Tamara. "Interview about Your Cell Phone
Service, Company, and History." Message

to the author. 21 Nov. 2011. E-mail.

Meehling, Rachel. "Interview about Your Cell Phone

Company, Service, and History." Message

to the author. 16 Nov. 2011. E-mail.

MetroPCS. "Check Voice Mail with Visual Voice Mail

from MetroPCS." Unlimited Wireless

Service - MetroPCS. MetroPCS, 2011. Web. 02

Nov. 2011.

MetroPCS. "Check Voice Mail with Visual Voice Mail

from MetroPCS." Unlimited Wireless

Service - MetroPCS. MetroPCS, 2011. Web. 02

Nov. 2011.

MetroPCS. "Download Music, Ringtones & Ringbacks."

Unlimited Wireless Service –

MetroPCS. MetroPCS, 2011. Web. 02 Nov. 2011.

MetroPCS. "Get Text, GPS, Email, and Downloads for Cell

Phones from MetroPCS." Unlimited

Wireless Service - MetroPCS. MetroPCS, 2011.

Web. 02 Nov. 2011.

MetroPCS. "MetroGUARD Deductibles." MetroPCS.

MetroPCS, 2011. Web. 2011.

MetroPCS. "MetroPCS | 4G LTE Frequently Asked

Questions." Unlimited Wireless Service –

MetroPCS. MetroPCS, 2011. Web. 02 Nov. 2011.

MetroPCS. "MetroPCS | Coverage." Unlimited Wireless

Service - MetroPCS. MetroPCS, 2011.

Web. 02 Nov. 2011. MetroPCS. "MetroPCS |

MetroPCS Family Plan FAQs." Unlimited Wireless Service

–

MetroPCS. MetroPCS, 2011. Web. 02 Nov. 2011.

MetroPCS. "MetroPCS | MetroPCS Flat Rate Cell Phone

Plans." Unlimited Wireless Service –

MetroPCS. MetroPCS, 2011. Web. 02 Nov. 2011.

MetroPCS. "MetroPCS - Pay Your Bill." Unlimited

Wireless Service - MetroPCS. MetroPCS.

Web. 30 Nov. 2011.

MetroPCS. "MetroPCS | Phones." Unlimited Wireless
Service - MetroPCS. MetroPCS, 2011.

   Web. 02 Nov. 2011.

MetroPCS. "MetroPCS | Rhapsody Free Trial." Unlimited
Wireless Service - MetroPCS.

   MetroPCS, 2011. Web. 02 Nov. 2011.

MetroPCS. "MetroPCS | ScreenIt." Unlimited Wireless
Service - MetroPCS. MetroPCS, 2011.

   Web. 02 Nov. 2011.

MetroPCS. "MetroPCS | TravelTalk." Unlimited Wireless
Service - MetroPCS. MetroPCS, 2011.

   Web. 02 Nov. 2011.

Rathbun, Lori. "Interview about Your Cell Phone
Company, Service, and History." Message to

   the author. 8 Nov. 2011. E-mail.

Reardon, Marguerite. "MetroPCS Launches First 4G LTE
Market and Phone | Signal Strength –

CNET News." *Technology News - CNET News.*

CNET, 21 Sept. 2011. Web. 29 Nov. 2011.

Simple Mobile. "OMG! SIMPLE Mobile | Coverage

Check." SIMPLE Mobile | Unlimited Cell

Phone Plans. Simple Mobile, 2011. Web. 03 Nov.

2011.

Simple Mobile. "OMG! SIMPLE Mobile | Coverage

Check." SIMPLE Mobile | Unlimited Cell

Phone Plans. Simple Mobile, 2011. Web. 03 Nov.

2011.

Simple Mobile. "OMG! SIMPLE Mobile | Coverage

Check." SIMPLE Mobile | Unlimited Cell

Phone Plans. Simple Mobile, 2011. Web. 03 Nov.

2011.

Simple Mobile. "OMG! SIMPLE Mobile | Coverage

Check." SIMPLE Mobile | Unlimited Cell

Phone Plans. Simple Mobile, 2011. Web. 03 Nov.

2011.

Simple Mobile. "Question about Your Fees and Insurance."

Message to the author. 4 Nov. 2011.

    E-mail.

Simple Mobile. "SIMPLE Mobile | 4G High Speed

Wireless Coverage." SIMPLE Mobile |

    Unlimited Cell Phone Plans. Simple Mobile, 2011.

    Web. 03 Nov. 2011.

Simple Mobile. "SIMPLE Mobile | About Us." SIMPLE

Mobile | Unlimited Cell Phone Plans.

    Simple Mobile, 2011. Web. 03 Nov. 2011.

Simple Mobile. "SIMPLE Mobile | International Long

Distance Rate." SIMPLE Mobile |

    Unlimited Cell Phone Plans. Simple Mobile, 2011.

    Web. 03 Nov. 2011.

Simple Mobile. "SIMPLE Mobile | Unlimited BlackBerry

Plans." SIMPLE Mobile | Unlimited

    Cell Phone Plans. Simple Mobile, 2011. Web. 03

    Nov. 2011.

Simple Mobile. "SIMPLE Mobile | Unlimited Talk, Text & High Speed Web." SIMPLE Mobile |

Unlimited Cell Phone Plans. Simple Mobile, 2011. Web. 03 Nov. 2011.

Simple Mobile. "SIMPLE Mobile | Unlimited Talk, Text & Web." SIMPLE Mobile | Unlimited

Cell Phone Plans. Simple Mobile, 2011. Web. 03 Nov. 2011.

Simple Mobile. "SIMPLE Mobile | Wireless Coverage Maps." SIMPLE Mobile | Unlimited Cell

Phone Plans. Simple Mobile, 2011. Web. 03 Nov. 2011.

Simple Mobile. "SIMPLE MOBILE Compatible All_Brands2 Phones." SIMPLE Mobile |

Unlimited Cell Phone Plans. Simple Mobile, 2011. Web. 02 Nov. 2011.

Simple Mobile. "SIMPLE MOBILE No-Contract-Plans: Unlocked-gsm-sim-card." SIMPLE

Mobile | Unlimited Cell Phone Plans. Simple

Mobile, 2011. Web. 03 Nov. 2011.

Sprint. "Care #20111102131138993 (Billing/Payment -

Payment Inquiries)

(KMM92545048V65030L0KM)." Message to the

author. 2 Nov. 2011. E-mail.

Sprint. "International Dialing from the U.S." Sprint. Sprint,

2011. Web. 5 Nov. 2011.

Sprint. "International Text from the U.S." Sprint. Sprint,

2011. Web. 5 Nov. 2011.

Sprint. "IPhone 4S 16GB." Sprint. Sprint, 2011. Web. 2

Nov. 2011.

Sprint. "Kyocera Brio." Sprint. Sprint, 2011. Web. 2 Nov.

2011.

Sprint. "LG Optimus S." Sprint. Sprint, 2011. Web. 2 Nov.

2011.

Sprint. "Simply Everything." Sprint. Sprint, 2011. Web. 5

Nov. 2011.

Sprint. "Simply Everything-Family." Sprint. Sprint, 2011.

Web. 5 Nov. 2011.

T-Mobile. "Cell Phone Coverage Maps For Your Calling

Coverage Areas | T-Mobile." Cell

Phones | 4G Cell Phone Plans | Android Tablet PCs

| T-Mobile. T-Mobile, 2011. Web. 04 Nov. 2011.

T-Mobile. "Cell Phone Coverage Maps For Your Calling

Coverage Areas | T-Mobile." Cell

Phones | 4G Cell Phone Plans | Android Tablet PCs

| T-Mobile. T-Mobile, 2011. Web. 05 Nov. 2011.

T-Mobile. "Cell Phone Plans | Rate Plans for Cell Phones |

T-Mobile." Cell Phones | 4G Cell

Phone Plans | Android Tablet PCs | T-Mobile. T-

Mobile, 2011. Web. 05 Nov. 2011.

T-Mobile. "Discount Family Cell Phone Plans | T-Mobile

Phone Plans for the Family." Cell

Phones | 4G Cell Phone Plans | Android Tablet PCs

| T-Mobile. T-Mobile, 2011. Web. 05 Nov. 2011.

T-Mobile. "HTC Sensation 4G Phone | Prices, Reviews &
Accessories | T-Mobile." Cell Phones |
4G Cell Phone Plans | Android Tablet PCs | T-
Mobile. T-Mobile, 2002-2011. Web. 02 Nov. 2011.

T-Mobile. "International Calling Rates." T-Mobile. T-
Mobile, 2011. Web. 4 Nov. 2011.

T-Mobile. "International Messaging Rates." Cell Phones |
4G Cell Phone Plans | Android Tablet
PCs | T-Mobile. T-Mobile, 2011. Web. 05 Nov.
2011.

T-Mobile. "International Roaming." Cell Phones | 4G Cell
Phone Plans | Android Tablet PCs | T-
Mobile. T-Mobile, 2011. Web. 05 Nov. 2011.

T-Mobile. "Monthly4G Prepaid Plans | Prepaid Data Plans |
T-Mobile." Prepaid Cell Phones |
No Contract Cell Phone Plans | T-Mobile. T-
Mobile, 2011. Web. 03 Nov. 2011.

T-Mobile. "Prepaid Cell Phone Coverage Map from T-Mobile." Prepaid Cell Phones |

> No Contract Cell Phone Plans | T-Mobile. T-Mobile, 2011. Web. 04 Nov. 2011.

T-Mobile. "Prepaid Cell Phone Plans | Additional Services| T-Mobile." Prepaid Cell Phones |

> No Contract Cell Phone Plans | T-Mobile. T-Mobile, 2011. Web. 04 Nov. 2011.

T-Mobile. "T-Mobile® Sidekick® 4G - Pearl Magenta - Refurbished Phone Details from

> T-Mobile." Cell Phones | 4G Cell Phone Plans | Android Tablet PCs | T-Mobile. T-Mobile, 2002-2011. Web. 02 Nov. 2011.

U.S. Cellular. "Device Insurance | Cell Phone Insurance | Features & Services | U.S. Cellular."

> U.S. Cellular | Cell Phone Plans | Cell Phone Service. U.S. Cellular, 2011. Web. 07 Nov. 2011.

U.S. Cellular. "Enter Location | U.S. Cellular Phones Plans

Offers | U.S. Cellular." U.S. Cellular |

Cell Phone Plans | Cell Phone Service. U.S.

Cellular, 2011. Web. 04 Nov. 2011.

U.S. Cellular. "Enter Location | U.S. Cellular Phones Plans

Offers | U.S. Cellular." U.S. Cellular |

Cell Phone Plans | Cell Phone Service. U.S.

Cellular, 2011. Web. 05 Nov. 2011.

U.S. Cellular. "Enter Location | U.S. Cellular Phones Plans

Offers | U.S. Cellular." U.S. Cellular |

Cell Phone Plans | Cell Phone Service. U.S.

Cellular, 2011. Web. 05 Nov. 2011.

U.S. Cellular. "HTC Merge™ | HTC Phones | Cell Phones |

U.S. Cellular." U.S. Cellular |

Cell Phone Plans | Cell Phone Service. U.S.

Cellular, 2011. Web. 04 Nov. 2011.

U.S. Cellular. "International Services | Features & Services

| U.S. Cellular." U.S. Cellular |

Cell Phone Plans | Cell Phone Service. U.S.

Cellular, 2011. Web. 05 Nov. 2011.

U.S. Cellular. "LG Optimus U™ | LG Phones | Cell Phones

| U.S. Cellular." U.S. Cellular |

Cell Phone Plans | Cell Phone Service. U.S.

Cellular, 2011. Web. 04 Nov. 2011.

U.S. Cellular. "LG Saber." U.S. Cellular. U.S. Cellular,

2011. Web. 2011.

U.S. Cellular. "Prepaid FAQs - Frequently Asked

Questions." U.S. Cellular. U.S. Cellular, 2011.

Web. 7 Nov. 2011.

U.S. Cellular. "Samsung Character™ - Blue | Samsung

Phones | Cell Phones | U.S. Cellular."

U.S. Cellular | Cell Phone Plans | Cell Phone

Service. U.S. Cellular, 2011. Web. 04 Nov. 2011.

U.S. Cellular. "Things We Want You To Know | U.S.

Cellular." U.S. Cellular | Cell Phone Plans

| Cell Phone Service. U.S. Cellular, 2011. Web. 07

Nov. 2011.

U.S. Cellular. "U.S. Cellular Coverage Indicator | Cell

Phone Coverage | U.S. Cellular." U.S.

Cellular | Cell Phone Plans | Cell Phone Service.

U.S. Cellular, 2011. Web. 05 Nov. 2011.

U.S. Cellular. "U.S. Cellular Voice And Data Maps | Cell

Phone Coverage | U.S. Cellular." U.S.

Cellular | Cell Phone Plans | Cell Phone Service.

U.S. Cellular, 2011. Web. 04 Nov. 2011.

U.S. Cellular. "Wireless Phone Insurance FAQs |

Frequently Asked Questions | U.S. Cellular."

U.S. Cellular | Cell Phone Plans | Cell Phone

Service. U.S. Cellular, 2011. Web. 07 Nov. 2011.

Verizon Wireless. "International Long Distance." Verizon

Wireless. Verizon Wireless, 2011.

Web. 2011.

Verizon Wireless. "International Picture & Video Messaging." Verizon Wireless. Verizon

    Wireless, 2011. Web. 5 Nov. 2011. <

Verizon Wireless. "International Text Messaging." Verizon Wireless. Verizon Wireless, 2011.

    Web. 5 Nov. 2011.

Verizon Wireless. "Other." Message to the author. 4 Nov. 2011. E-mail.

Verizon Wireless. "Pantech Breakout." Cell Phones - Smartphones: Cell Phone Service,

    Accessories - Verizon Wireless. Verizon Wireless, 2011. Web. 02 Nov. 2011.

Verizon Wireless. "Plans - Verizon Wireless." Cell Phones - Smartphones: Cell Phone Service,

    Accessories - Verizon Wireless. Verizon Wireless, 2011. Web. 04 Nov. 2011.

Verizon Wireless. "Plans - Verizon Wireless." Cell Phones - Smartphones: Cell Phone Service,

Accessories - Verizon Wireless. Verizon Wireless,

2011. Web. 05 Nov. 2011.

Verizon Wireless. "Plans - Verizon Wireless." Cell Phones

- Smartphones: Cell Phone Service,

Accessories - Verizon Wireless. Verizon Wireless,

2011. Web. 05 Nov. 2011.

Verizon Wireless. "Prepaid Cell Phone Plans | Verizon

Wireless." Cell Phones - Smartphones:

Cell Phone Service, Accessories - Verizon Wireless.

Verizon Wireless, 2011. Web. 07 Nov. 2011.

Verizon Wireless. "Prepaid International Services."

Verizon Wireless. Verizon Wireless, 2011.

Web. 4 Nov. 2011.

Verizon Wireless. "Rates & Coverage." Verizon Wireless.

Verizon Wireless, 2011. Web. 5 Nov.

2011.

Verizon Wireless. "Return Policy & Termination Fee |

Verizon Wireless." Cell Phones –

Smartphones: Cell Phone Service, Accessories -

Verizon Wireless. Verizon Wireless, 2011. Web. 07

Nov. 2011.

Verizon Wireless. "Samsung Stratosphere." Cell Phones -

Smartphones: Cell Phone Service,

Accessories - Verizon Wireless. Verizon Wireless,

2011. Web. 02 Nov. 2011.

Verizon Wireless. "Verizon Wireless - Explore." Cell

Phones - Smartphones: Cell Phone

Service, Accessories - Verizon Wireless. Verizon

Wireless, 2011. Web. 05 Nov. 2011.

Virgin Mobile. "Cell Phone Plans - Pay As You Go and

Prepaid | Virgin Mobile." Prepaid Cell

Phone Service and Pay as You Go | Virgin Mobile.

Virgin Mobile, 2011. Web. 02 Nov. 2011.

Virgin Mobile. "Other." Message to the author. 2 Nov.

2011. E-mail.

Virgin Mobile. "Phone Insurance." Virgin Mobile. Virgin

Mobile. Web. 5 Nov. 2011.

Virgin Mobile. "Virgin Mobile USA." Prepaid Cell Phone

Service and Pay as You Go

    | Virgin Mobile. Virgin Mobile, 2011. Web. 05

    Nov. 2011.